CW00689667

MOURNING

The Prelude to Laughter

Bonnie Bruno

ZondervanPublishingHouse

Grand Rapids, Michigan

A Division of HarperCollins*Publishers*

Contents

The Beatitude Series

Welcome to the Beatitude Series. This series is designed to help you develop the eight character qualities found in those whom Jesus calls "blessed."

The Beatitudes are among the best-known and best-loved words of Jesus. They form the heart of the Sermon on the Mount, found in Matthew 5–7 and Luke 6:17–49. In eight brief statements Jesus describes the lifestyle that God desires and rewards:

> *Blessed are the poor in spirit,*
> * for theirs is the kingdom of heaven.*
> *Blessed are those who mourn,*
> * for they will be comforted.*
> *Blessed are the meek,*
> * for they will inherit the earth.*
> *Blessed are those who hunger and thirst for righteousness,*
> * for they will be filled.*

Blessed are the merciful,
for they will be shown mercy.
Blessed are the pure in heart,
for they will see God.
Blessed are the peacemakers,
for they will be called sons of God.
Blessed are those who are persecuted because of righteousness,
for theirs is the kingdom of heaven.

The Beatitudes turn the world's values upside down. We are tempted to say: "*Wretched* are the poor, for they have so little money. *Wretched* are those who mourn, for no one will hear their cries. *Wretched* are the meek, for they will be trampled by the powerful." Yet Jesus shatters our stereotypes and asserts that the poor will be rich, the mourners will be comforted, and the meek will inherit everything. What a strange kingdom he offers!

In recent years there has been some confusion about the kind of blessing Christ promises in these verses. The Beatitudes have been described as "God's prescription for happiness." One book has even called them "The Be-Happy Attitudes."

The Greek word *makarios* can mean "happy." J. B. Phillips translates the opening words of each beatitude, "How happy are . . . !" Nevertheless, John Stott writes:

> It is seriously misleading to render *makarios* "happy." For happiness is a subjective state, whereas Jesus is making an objective judgment about these people. He is declaring not what they may feel like ("happy"), but what God thinks of them and what on that account they are: they are "blessed."[1]

The eight guides in the Beatitude Series give you an in-depth look at each beatitude. But Jesus is not describing eight different types of people—some who are meek, others who are merciful, and still others who are peacemakers. He desires to see all eight character qualities in every one of his followers.

That's a tall order! Only those who enter Christ's kingdom by faith can expect such a transformation. And only those who serve the King can enjoy his rewards.

Our prayer is that The Beatitude Series will give you a clearer and deeper grasp of what it truly means to be blessed.

HOW TO USE THE BEATITUDE SERIES

The Beatitude Series is designed to be flexible. You can use the guides in any order that is best for you or your group. They are ideal for Sunday-school classes, small groups, one-on-one relationships, or as materials for your quiet times.

Because each guide contains only six studies, you can easily explore more than one beatitude. In a Sunday-school class, any two guides can be combined for a quarter (twelve weeks), or the entire series can be covered in a year.

Each study deliberately focuses on a limited number of passages, usually only one or two. That allows you to see each passage in its context, avoiding the temptation of prooftexting and the frustration of "Bible hopscotch" (jumping from verse to verse). If you would like to look up additional passages, a Bible concordance will give the most help.

The Beatitude Series helps you *discover* what the Bible says rather than simply *telling* you the answers. The questions encourage you to think and to explore options rather than merely to fill in the blanks with one-word answers.

Leader's notes are provided in the back of each guide. They show how to lead a group discussion, provide additional information on questions, and suggest ways to deal with problems that may come up in the discussion. With such helps, someone with little or no experience can lead an effective study.

SUGGESTIONS FOR INDIVIDUAL STUDY

1. Begin each study with prayer. Ask God to help you understand the passage and to apply it to your life.

2. A good modern translation, such as the *New International Version,* the *New American Standard Bible,* or the *New Revised Standard Version,* will give you the most help. Questions in this guide, however, are based on the *New International Version.*

3. Read and reread the passage(s). You must know what the passage says before you can understand what it means and how it applies to you.

4. Write your answers in the space provided in the study guide. This will help you to clearly express your understanding of the passage.

5. Keep a Bible dictionary handy. Use it to look up any unfamiliar words, names, or places.

SUGGESTIONS FOR GROUP STUDY

1. Come to the study prepared. Careful preparation will greatly enrich your time in group discussion.

2. Be willing to join in the discussion. The leader of the group will not be lecturing but will encourage people to discuss what they have learned in the passage. Plan to share what God has taught you in your individual study.

3. Stick to the passage being studied. Base your answers on the verses being discussed rather than on outside authorities such as commentaries or your favorite author or speaker.

4. Try to be sensitive to the other members of the group. Listen attentively when they speak, and be affirming whenever you can. This will encourage more hesitant members of the group to participate.

5. Be careful not to dominate the discussion. By all means participate! But allow others to have equal time.

6. If you are the discussion leader, you will find additional suggestions and helpful ideas in the leader's notes at the back of the guide.

Note

1. *The Message of the Sermon on the Mount* (Downers Grove, Ill.: InterVarsity Press, 1978), p. 33.

Introducing Mourning

Blessed are those who mourn,
for they will be comforted.

I love a good thunderstorm. How it forms and why one passes by so quickly while another has the fury to snap trees like matchsticks are a source of mystery to me.

I've awakened in the middle of the night to thunder that rumbled like a runaway train. Family campouts have been interrupted by howling winds, relentless rain, and lightning that drove us hurrying down our mountaintop retreat back to the safety of home.

Thunderstorms have played a worthwhile role in my life, too. As a very young child, I learned to look beyond the thunderclaps to the One who spoke to the wind, calmed the most turbulent sea, and heard my whispers even above the crackle of lightning. Because I learned to trust God in the middle of such storms, I was never saddled with a fear of thunder, as were many of my playmates.

Instead of rushing in a panic to my parents, I'd sit and press my face against the bedroom window to watch the heavenly display of fireworks. Even when our electricity flickered and went out, I'd be the one enjoying the coziness of huddling in the dark, listening to the wind whistling through the trees.

Life is full of the unexpected, isn't it? Sudden storms roar into our lives, often leaving sorrow and destruction in their wake. And that's exactly what this book is about—storms, their aftermath, and the hope that believers can cling to confidently in the midst of a seemingly hopeless situation.

Our study will explore the legitimacy of mourning, plus the cleansing that springs from it. We'll take a look at Bible characters whose journeys through depression and grief have been recorded to help us weather our own personal storms. Our study will also touch upon God's deliverance as he guides us safely through the low points of our lives, as well as the everlasting joy that will be ours to enjoy in his presence.

Whether you're midway through a storm, recovering from one, or anticipating bad weather on the horizon, this guide has been written especially for you.

Bonnie Bruno

1

A Time to Mourn

ECCLESIASTES 7:1 – 6

During the Vietnam War, many soldiers described their experiences as a period of drastic growth. One young man wrote a letter home, saying that he felt "like an old man who'd lost touch with the 19-year-old who used to be." Another expressed a sudden interest in getting to know God, "just in case I have to meet Him soon."

A time of loss can be devastating. But it can also give us the opportunity, with God's help, to persevere and grow spiritually. In Ecclesiastes 7:1 – 6, Solomon shares some wise advice about examining the direction of our lives while there is yet time.

1. Do you tend to feel closer to the Lord in difficult times or when things are going well? Explain.

2. Read Ecclesiastes 7:1 – 6. In what ways might a good name be like—and better than—fine perfume (v. 1)?

3. How might the day of a person's death be better than the day of his or her birth (v. 1)?

4. What things can we learn during a time of mourning that might be overlooked in happier days (vv. 2 – 3)?

5. Do you ever feel resentful when things aren't going well? Explain. (See also 7:14.)

6. The "heart" (v. 4) denotes the inner person; the seat of all thoughts and desires. How can seeking pleasure keep a person from facing his mortality?

How would you advise someone who says that he or she has "plenty of time" to think about eternity?

7. Can you recall a "wise" person who took the time to give you a "rebuke" (v. 5)? What was your reaction?

8. Although a peron's rebuke can make us mourn over our sin, how might our sorrow produce godly results (see 2 Cor. 7:8 – 13)?

9. Has the fear of rejection ever kept you from offering sound advice to a friend or loved one? Explain.

10. Thorns burn quickly, make a lot of noise, and die out. Why does Solomon compare the crackling of thorns to the "laughter of fools" (v. 6)?

Why is the laughter of fools "meaningless"?

11. Solomon urges us to realize that sadness, sorrow, and mourning are often better than parties, songs, and laughter. Why is this such a difficult message for us to accept?

12. Pray that hardships and sorrows will deepen your character and increase your awareness of how short life is. Ask for grace to live in light of eternity.

MEMORY VERSE

It is better to go to a house of mourning than to go to a house of feasting, for death is the destiny of every man; the living should take this to heart.

Ecclesiastes 7:2

BETWEEN STUDIES

To help you better understand the role that heartache and loss have played in your life, jot down any related memories that stand out. Think about what you've learned from each experience and thank God for his faithfulness through them.

In the following passages, you can read about Bible characters who grieved for their lost loved ones:

❑ Abraham: Genesis 23:1–4

❑ Jacob: Genesis 37:34–35

❑ Israelites: Deuteronomy 34:7–8

❑ David: 2 Samuel 1:11–12

Psalm 126:5–6 offers hope for the person whose heart is breaking. See if you can locate three more passages that would be of help.

2

Good Grief

1 SAMUEL 1:1–2:11

Corrie ten Boom's imprisonment in a concentration camp, loss of loved ones, and her eventual homegoing is a story of courage and ultimate victory in Christ. Saddled by grief and uncertainty, Corrie still exhibited a love for her fellow prisoners and even her oppressors that could only have come from God himself.

Without grief, who would ever experience the wonder of God's sustaining grace? Without rain, would any of us fully appreciate the sunshine?

In the first two chapters of 1 Samuel, we see the positive results that come when we entrust our grief to God.

1. What thoughts and images come to mind when you hear the word *grief?*

2. Read 1 Samuel 1. How is the situation described in verses 1–2 a recipe for conflict and grief?

3. What, in your opinion, motivated Penninnah to provoke and irritate Hannah (vv. 6–8)?

4. How does Hannah react to Penninnah's ridicule (v. 7)?

How would you have handled the situation?

5. In what ways was Elkanah an encouraging husband?

6. Hannah's grief reaches its peak in verses 10–11. What does her vow (v. 11) tell us about her relationship with God?

7. Eli reacts harshly to Hannah's anguished prayer (vv. 12–14). How does Hannah respond (vv. 15–16)?

8. How do you respond when someone fails to understand your grief?

9. Eli's heart softens in verse 17. What does his reply say about his faith in God?

10. How do we know that Hannah had turned her situation totally over to God (v. 18)?

How can entrusting our situation to God give us hope in the midst of grief?

11. Read 1 Samuel 2:1–11. In 1:24–28, Hannah gave up her beloved firstborn, yet chapter 2 begins with rejoicing. Do these two actions sound incompatible to you? Why?

12. What does Hannah's prayer reveal about the Lord and the surprising reversals he brings about?

In what ways has God turned your grief into joy or your weakness into strength?

MEMORY VERSE

He raises the poor from the dust and lifts the needy from the ash heap; he seats them with princes and has them inherit a throne of honor.

1 Samuel 2:8

BETWEEN STUDIES

Read the passages listed below. How do the characters' attitudes compare to the way you react to life's trials?

- ❏ Genesis 50:10–11: Joseph gives himself permission to grieve
- ❏ Job 1:8–22; 2:3–10: Job draws strength from God
- ❏ John 11:17–37: Martha and Mary blame Jesus

The following passages were written to strengthen us in times of sorrow: Isaiah 40:31; 2 Corinthians 12:9; Hebrews 2:18; James 1:2–4; and 1 Peter 1:7. Why not share them today by sending a note to someone who needs encouragement?

3

Hope for the Troubled

PSALM 42

An eleven-year-old boy spent a harrowing ninety minutes in a runaway hot-air balloon, whizzing across a Colorado forest. Convinced that he'd never touch ground again, he turned to a CB radio for help. An experienced balloonist happened to have his CB on and heard the boy's desperate cries. Over the next hour, he calmly guided the boy into an open field.

When troubling circumstances interrupt our lives, we must act quickly. We must turn our troubles over to the God who has already promised to guide and deliver us.

Psalm 42 is a source of encouragement for the troubled heart as it urges us to put our hope in God.

1. Describe a time when you felt as helpless as the boy in the runaway balloon.

2. Read Psalm 42. During troubled times, how does your longing for God compare to extreme thirst (vv. 1–2)?

3. What words and phrases indicate the depth of the psalmist's sorrow?

4. Sorrow has its rightful place, yet it becomes a problem if allowed to control us. How would you describe the psalmist's outlook in verses 4–6?

5. The psalmist makes himself remember God's faithfulness in the past (vv. 4, 6). How can the memory of past answers to prayer encourage us and give us hope?

6. Think of a time when you chose to "put your hope in God" (v. 5) in the midst of your troubling circumstances. How did it affect your general outlook?

Now think of a situation in which you became immersed in self-pity. How did it compare to the previous situation?

7. The psalmist's troubles feel like "waves and breakers" sweeping over him (v. 7). How might such overwhelming feelings erode a Christian's confidence in God?

8. We could call verse 8 the psalmist's "statement of faith." What are some ways God "directs his love" toward you by day and at night?

How can verse 8 be a comfort to someone who's feeling overwhelmed by problems?

9. The writer of verse 8 launches immediately into a description of his despair in verses 9–10. Do you consider this a contradiction? Explain.

10. The psalmist speaks of being pressured by the opinions of his "foes" (v. 10). How well do you deal with others who ridicule your Christian convictions?

11. The last verse of Psalm 42 brings us full circle, as the psalmist declares his trust in God. Why do you think God allows trouble into our lives?

What memorable things has God done in the past that can give you hope in troubled times?

12. Ask God to increase your sensitivity to the struggles of others. Pray for practical ways to encourage others, especially those who may be suffering secretly.

MEMORY VERSE

By day the LORD directs his love, at night his song is with me— a prayer to the God of my life.

Psalm 42:8

BETWEEN STUDIES

Make a list of problems that you've experienced during the past year. Meditate on the lessons you've learned from each and thank God for his love and faithfulness.

Read the following passages for further insight into God's help for the troubled:

- ❑ Jonah 2:1–10
- ❑ 2 Corinthians 1:8–10
- ❑ Psalm 116:1–9

4

A Time to Dance

PSALM 30

A little girl was looking forward to beginning preschool in the fall. Before registration, however, she would need several dreaded immunizations.

"It'll only sting for a couple of seconds," assured the nurse. The girl squeezed her eyes closed and hummed a favorite chorus as loudly as she could. In fact, she was so caught up in avoiding the sting of the needle that she hummed right through the immunization!

Psalm 30 presents a picture of relief and celebration. The worst is now over, and the psalmist rejoices in the realization that God has delivered him.

1. Have you ever felt so caught up in the pain of an event that you found it difficult to look ahead to its resolution? Explain.

2. Read Psalm 30. What words would you use to describe the mood of this psalm?

3. How does David's vivid imagery ("depths," "grave," "pit") help us understand his predicament (vv. 1–3)?

4. David says, "I called to you for help" (v. 2). When things go wrong, do you ever try to work them out yourself before calling on God? Explain.

5. Why might God sometimes withhold his help until we ask him for it?

6. In verse 1 David had said, "I will exalt you, O LORD." Why does he now invite God's saints to join him in praise (vv. 4–5)?

7. A night of "weeping" feels as though it will last forever (v. 5). How does verse 5 put the "nights" of our lives in proper perspective?

8. Describe a time when God gave you (or someone you were praying for) the joy of morning after a nighttime of suffering.

9. What do verses 6 and 7 tell us about David's sense of security?

Why do you think the Lord hid his face from David (v. 7)?

10. Verse 9 almost sounds as if David was trying to bargain with God. Have you ever tried to sway God's decision? Explain.

11. According to *The New Bible Dictionary,* "mercy" (vv. 8, 10) is "the gracious favor of the superior to the inferior, all undeserved." How does this definition help you to better understand David's plea in verses 8 and 10?

12. In what ways do verses 11–12 present a beautiful example of gratitude and praise?

13. Take a moment to thank God for his gracious dealings in your life. Thank him, too, for the lessons he has taught you through trials.

MEMORY VERSE

For his anger lasts only a moment, but his favor lasts a lifetime; weeping may remain for a night, but rejoicing comes in the morning.

Psalm 30:5

BETWEEN STUDIES

A disciplined Bible study and prayer time can prepare us for future difficulties. Spiritual discipline also enables us to give credit to God in times of deliverance.

During your Bible study and prayer time, read all of Psalm 119. This is the longest psalm, and one that will help you reflect on all that God has done in your life. If you wish, highlight those verses that speak of God's faithfulness.

5

No More Tears

REVELATION 21:1–8

A famous tightrope walker was reminiscing about his boy-hood in the circus. He remembered that when it was his turn to walk the high wire, his legs shook uncontrollably.

An older family member recognized the boy's fear and took him aside. "Just look straight ahead," he advised, "and never down. Think only of the next step."

Revelation 21:1–8 gives us a glimpse of a future so glorious it is almost hard to grasp. Through this study, we'll discover the peace that is ours when we look beyond today to an eternity in God's presence.

1. When you try to imagine a "perfect world," what images come to mind?

2. Read Revelation 21:1–8. As John describes the new heaven and the new earth, what details appeal to you most? Why?

3. The "new Jerusalem" (v. 2) signifies the church of God. Why does John compare the church to a city and to a bride?

4. A dramatic change will take place with the arrival of the new Jerusalem—God promises to live among his people for eternity (v. 3). Why do you think the God of the universe wants to live with us?

5. God also promises to remove all "death or mourning or crying or pain" (v. 4). Would this verse be a help or a hindrance to someone who is mourning? Why?

6. John's vision took place centuries before the new Jerusalem would be established (v. 5). Why do you think John was asked to record this vision?

What effect does this vision have on your life?

7. Why are God's titles ("the Alpha and the Omega," "the Beginning and the End") stressed in verse 6?

8. Who will receive the promises of John's vision, and who will not—and why (vv. 6–8; see also, v. 27)?

9. What is meant by "thirsty" in verse 6 (see also Isa. 55:1)?

10. What does it mean to be an overcomer (v. 7)?

Do you think God sees you as an overcomer? Explain.

11. Why do you think "cowardice" and "unbelief" are listed first in verse 8?

12. What is meant by "the second death" (v. 8b)?

Why do you think John adds this warning to his vision of the new Jerusalem?

13. Ask God to increase your thirst for the waters of life. Pray for the strength to overcome every obstacle in your path to the new Jerusalem.

MEMORY VERSE

He will wipe every tear from their eyes. There will be no more death or mourning or crying or pain, for the old order of things has passed away.

Revelation 21:4

BETWEEN STUDIES

Write the names of three people who have not yet asked Christ to be their Savior. Pray for opportunities to share your testimony with them, and thank God for providing a means of securing eternal life with him

To better understand John's vision of the new Jerusalem, read about the road that leads to it:

❑ John 16:33

❑ Romans 8:18–27

❑ 1 Thessalonians 5:8–10

Being a believer does not mean that we'll never cry again. The following verses speak of tears and their cleansing effect:

❑ Psalm 126:5

❑ Isaiah 25:8

❑ Jeremiah 31:16

❑ 2 Corinthians 2:4

6

Everlasting Joy

ISAIAH 61:1–7

The first half of the 19th century found Americans searching for the highly acclaimed "good life." Farmers drifted away from rural areas to seek their fortunes in booming cities. The standard of living rose so quickly that almost everyone set their sights on bigger, better homes furnished with indoor plumbing, cooking stoves, bathtubs, and ready-made furniture. Happiness could be bought—or so it seemed.

Isaiah 61:1–7 describes the endless wealth that is ours as believers. This passage reveals that true and lasting happiness is not dependent on power, position, or possessions.

1. How much does your contentment fluctuate with life's ups and downs? Explain.

2. Read Isaiah 61:1–7. Who are the "poor," "brokenheart-ed," "captives," and "prisoners" (v. 1)?

Do any of those descriptions apply to you or someone you know? Explain.

3. How is "the year of the LORD's favor" (v. 2) similar to the Year of Jubilee described in Leviticus 25:8–12, 39–43?

4. How do you envision the "day of vengeance of our God" (v. 2)?

Does the thought frighten you? Explain.

5. How do the images of "crown," "oil," and "garment" (v. 3) give a beautiful portrait of Christ's comfort for those who mourn?

6. When have you experienced the beauty of putting on a "garment of praise" after a time of despair?

7. Why is "oaks of righteousness" (v. 3) a good way to describe the character of God's people?

8. When we grow strong in Christ and experience his healing touch, how does that display God's splendor (v. 3)?

9. In what ways do you see God's splendor displayed in your life?

10. Verse 4 describes a period of rebuilding, restoration, and renewal. How does this apply to the one who has received Christ as Savior and Lord?

11. Under the New Covenant, every believer is declared a priest and a minister (v. 6; see also 1 Pet. 2:4). What opportunities do you have to minister to those in your church, at work, or in your neighborhood?

12. Are you ever hesitant about allowing others to minister to your needs, or do you readily accept their help as God's provision? Explain.

13. The firstborn son received a double portion of the inheritance from his father (v. 7). How would you describe your "inheritance" to a nonbeliever?

14. Ask God to give you a foretaste of the everlasting joy that is yours in Christ.

MEMORY VERSE

Instead of their shame my people will receive a double portion, and instead of disgrace they will rejoice in their inheritance; and so they will inherit a double portion in their land, and everlasting joy will be theirs.

Isaiah 61:7

BETWEEN STUDIES

For further study, read the following passages which describe your inheritance in Christ:

- ❑ Matthew 5:5; 19:29; 25:34
- ❑ Ephesians 1:13–14
- ❑ Colossians 1:12; 3:23–24
- ❑ Hebrews 9:15
- ❑ 1 Peter 1:3–4

Paul's hope never wavered, even though he experienced severe hardships during his ministry. You can read about how he responded to some of those hardships in Philippians 1:12–30, 2 Timothy 1:12–18, and 4:16–18.

Make a list of "What if . . ." situations. Think ahead to how you would cope with God's help.

Leader's Notes

Leading a Bible discussion—especially for the first time—can make you feel both nervous and excited. If you are nervous, realize that you are in good company. Many biblical leaders, such as Moses, Joshua, and the apostle Paul, felt nervous and inadequate to lead others (see, for example, 1 Corinthians 2:3). Yet God's grace was sufficient for them, just as it will be for you.

Some excitement is also natural. Your leadership is a gift to the others in the group. Keep in mind, however, that other group members also share responsibility for the group. Your role is simply to stimulate discussion by asking questions and encouraging people to respond. The suggestions listed below can help you to be an effective leader.

PREPARING TO LEAD

1. Ask God to help you understand and apply the passage to your own life. Unless that happens, you will not be prepared to lead others.

2. Carefully work through each question in the study guide. Meditate and reflect on the passage as you formulate your answers.

3. Familiarize yourself with the leader's notes for the study. These will help you understand the purpose of the study and will provide valuable information about the questions in the study.

4. Pray for the various members of the group. Ask God to use these studies to make you better disciples of Jesus Christ.

5. Before the first meeting, make sure each person has a study guide. Encourage them to prepare beforehand for each study.

LEADING THE STUDY

1. Begin the study on time. If people realize that the study begins on schedule, they will work harder to arrive on time.

2. At the beginning of your first time together, explain that these studies are designed to be discussions, not lectures. Encourage everyone to participate, but realize that some may be hesitant to speak during the first few sessions.

3. Read the introductory paragraph at the beginning of the discussion. This will orient the group to the passage being studied.

4. Read the passage aloud. You may choose to do this yourself, or you might ask for volunteers.

5. The questions in the guide are designed to be used just as they are written. If you wish, you may simply read each one aloud to the group. Or you may prefer to express them in your own words. Unnecessary rewording of the questions, however, is not recommended.

6. Don't be afraid of silence. People in the group may need time to think before responding.

7. Avoid answering your own questions. If necessary, rephrase a question until it is clearly understood. Even an

eager group will quickly become passive and silent if they think the leader will do most of the talking.

8. Encourage more than one answer to each question. Ask, "What do the rest of you think?" or "Anyone else?" until several people have had a chance to respond.

9. Try to be affirming whenever possible. Let people know you appreciate their insights into the passage.

10. Never reject an answer. If it is clearly wrong, ask, "Which verse led you to that conclusion?" Or let the group handle the problem by asking them what they think about the question.

11. Avoid going off on tangents. If people wander off course, gently bring them back to the passage being considered.

12. Conclude your time together with conversational prayer. Ask God to help you apply those things that you learned in the study.

13. End on time. This will be easier if you control the pace of the discussion by not spending too much time on some questions or too little on others.

Many more suggestions and helps are found in the book *Leading Bible Discussions* (InterVarsity Press). Reading it would be well worth your time.

STUDY 1
A Time to Mourn
ECCLESIASTES 7:1–6

Purpose: To discover how sorrow can lead us into a deeper relationship with God.

Question 1 Every study begins with an "approach question," which is discussed *before* reading the passage. An approach question is designed to do three things.

First, it helps to break the ice. Because an approach question doesn't require any knowledge of the passage or any special preparation, it can get people talking and can help them to warm up to each other.

Second, an approach question can motivate people to study the passage at hand. At the beginning of the study, people in the group aren't necessarily ready to jump into the world of the Bible. Their minds may be on other things (their kids, a problem at work, an upcoming meeting) that have nothing to do with the study. An approach question can capture their interest and draw them into the discussion by raising important issues related to the study. The question becomes a bridge between their personal lives and the answers found in Scripture.

Third, a good approach question can reveal where people's thoughts or feelings need to be transformed by Scripture. That is why it is important to ask the approach question *before* reading the passage. The passage might inhibit the spontaneous, honest answers people might have given, because they feel compelled to give biblical answers. The approach question allows them to compare their personal thoughts and feelings with what they later discover in Scripture.

Question 2 In Bible times, perfume was a valuable product of trade. Even the poorest kept at least a small amount of perfume and oil in their home. Some of their uses included: to mask body odor, soften the skin, prepare bodies for burial, and anoint the head of a guest of honor.

When Jewish parents named their offspring, they carefully selected a name to reflect the character of a loved one; the circumstances of birth; as a promise to God; or, in some cases, as a description of the type of person they hoped the child would become.

The name of Jesus is elevated throughout the New Testament to reflect his trustworthiness. (See Matthew 1:21; 18:20; John 14:13; Romans 10:13; Philippians 2:10; and Colossians 3:17.)

Question 4 Because we naturally gravitate toward pleasant experiences, verse 3 may sound rather confusing. (Why would sorrow be "better than laughter"?)

Keep the group's focus on what might be learned as a result of sorrow, rather than on a discussion of which experience is preferable.

We can learn lasting lessons from our sorrow. Take a moment as a group to quietly reflect on such an experience. See if one or two would like to share what they've learned through sorrow. If time permits, look up the following related passages:

- Godly sorrow brings repentance: 2 Corinthians 7:10
- Sorrow compared to childbirth: John 16:21–22
- Sorrow strengthens faith: 1 Peter 1:3–8

Laughter is fleeting and may even be used at times as a cover-up for our true feelings (Prov. 14:13).

Questions 7–9 Our reaction to criticism ("rebuke") reveals the level of our spiritual maturity. Discuss why criticism often hurts rather than helps.

Prior to the study, look up the following verses to discover more about giving and receiving criticism:

- 2 Samuel 12:5–13; 16:10–12
- Psalm 141:5
- Proverbs 9:7–9
- Matthew 7:1–5
- Luke 17:3–4
- Romans 2:21–22
- 2 Corinthians 7:8–13
- Galatians 5:14–15

STUDY 2
Good Grief
1 SAMUEL 1:1–2:11

Purpose: To realize that our grief can provide an opportunity to experience God's faithfulness.

Questions 2–3 Although polygamy was often practiced in the Old Testament, it usually led to conflict and grief. (See, for example, Genesis 29:31–30:24.) And because children were viewed as a sign of God's blessing, being childless was considered a disgrace.

Question 5 As you talk about Elkanah, you may wish to discuss ways to minister to those who may be experiencing a time of grief.

Question 6 Part of Hannah's promise, in exchange for a son, was to dedicate her child to God's service. Samuel's commitment was for life—in contrast to the normal twenty-five years of service for Levites (Num. 8:23–26).

Some Bible scholars believe that Hannah was taking a vow for her unborn son as part of the Nazirite tradition (see Num. 6:1–21). Called a "Nazirite vow," it was a commitment before God that was considered sacred. That would explain her promise that "no razor will ever be used on his head," because the person mentioned in the Nazirite vow was not to cut his hair as long as the covenant was in effect (usually for a limited period of time rather than for life).

Question 7 "Eli's mistake suggests that in those days it was not uncommon for drunken people to enter the sanctuary. Further evidence of the religious and moral deterioration of the time is found in the stories of Judges 17–21" (*The NIV Study Bible* [Grand Rapids, Mich.: Zondervan, 1885], p. 375).

Question 10 Perhaps because Eli was the Lord's priest, Hannah believed that his word ("May the God of Israel grant you what you have asked of him") was all the assurance she needed. Her conviction that her prayer would be answered is seen in the fact that she finally ate something, and her face was no longer downcast (v. 18).

Question 11 "Hannah's prayer is a song of praise and thanksgiving to God . . . This song has sometimes been termed the

'Magnificat of the OT' because it is so similar to the Magnificat of the NT (Mary's song, Lk 1:46–55). It also has certain resemblances to the 'Benedictus' (the song of Zechariah, Lk 1:67–79). . . . The supreme source of Hannah's joy is not in the child, but in the God who has answered her prayer" (*The NIV Study Bible*, p. 376).

STUDY 3
Hope for the Troubled
PSALM 42

Purpose: To understand that God is our light at the end of every dark tunnel.

Question 2 A deer will "pant" for water when he has an immediate thirst to quench. This psalm was written for those who thirst for God during times of depression or loneliness.

Other passages that mention intense thirst are John 4:10, 13–15 and 7:37–39.

Question 3 Notice such phrases as "My tears have been my food day and night" (v. 3), "I pour out my soul" (v. 4), "Why are you so downcast" (v. 4), "all your waves and breakers have swept over me" (v. 7), and so on.

Questions 4–5 "The psalmist analyzes his feelings and asks questions of himself (vv. 5, 11; 43:5). . . . The inner feelings express themselves in questions, despair, and hope in God. The questions are overtaking him. Yet, while hemmed in by the questions in his desperate situation, he still could engage himself in dialog. There was no voice from God. In the loneliness of alienation, his faith was tried and triumphed! Faith and doubt are twins; and when doubt seemed to triumph, true faith calmed its questions. . . . Hope, in essence, is waiting for God to act (cf. 38:15; 39:7). Hope is focused on the glorious acts of salvation and victory of which the Law, Historical Writings, and Prophets speak" (Willem A. VanGemeren, *Psalms,* The Expositor's Bible Commentary [Grand Rapids, Mich.: Zondervan, 1991], p. 333).

Ask the group to think of a time when praise and remembrance lifted them out of despair.

For related psalms, see the following: Psalm 71:14; 73:26; 116:5–6; 146:6–8.

Questions 8–9 "Above all, verse 8 is as deeply assured of God's presence as verses 9f. are hurt by His 'absence' . . . There is no easing of the stress, but the emotions now have the background of strong convictions. So there is a telling contrast between the mentions of *day . . . and . . . night* in verse 8 and verse 3" (Derek Kidner, *Psalms 1–72* [Downers Grove, Ill.: InterVarsity Press, 1973], p. 167).

STUDY 4
A Time to Dance
PSALM 30

Purpose: To emphasize that hard times are temporary, but God's love and care belong to Christians for eternity.

Question 2 "The vividness of ["you lifted me out of the depths"] is quite accurate: it is the word for pulling up a bucket from a well. That well was as deep as death . . . and the threat had come from sickness (2b) rather than war" (Kidner, *Psalms,* p. 128).

Question 4 While independence is admirable in some cases (for example, an older child getting ready to leave home for the first time, or a Christian standing against peer pressure), the Bible exhorts, "Seek the Lord while he may be found; call on him while he is near" (Isa. 55:6). We need God's wisdom, counsel, and guidance to be effective servants.

The following verses describe a proper dependence on God:

- Psalm 62:8; 105:4; 116:1–2
- Proverbs 1:29–33; 12:15; 28:14
- Isaiah 56:11; 59:10

Question 6 Because of God's covenant of grace, we can be assured that his favor will follow his anger, once we've repented and asked his forgiveness. It is an ongoing process, not a one-time event. True happiness depends on God's favor.

You may wish to compare God's forgiveness of us with the parent-child relationship.

Question 11 Jesus teaches about mercy in Matthew 18:23–35. As preparation for this study, read that passage and be prepared to point out how it illustrates the principal of mercy.

Question 13 This would be a good time to share testimonies of God's deliverance. Be sure to praise God not only for what he has done but also for who he is.

STUDY 5
No More Tears
REVELATION 21:1–8

Purpose: To realize that we can cling to the hope of a glorious eternity with Christ, free of sorrow and pain.

Question 1 Some people may give humorous answers to this question ("no dishes to wash," "no dirty diapers," and so on). Let them have their fun (it's good for the group), but ask for some serious answers, too.

Question 3 "John calls the city a 'bride' (cf. 21:9; 22:17). . . . The multiple imagery is needed to portray the tremendous reality of the city. A bride-city captures something of God's personal relationship to his people (the bride) as well as something of their life in communion with him and one another (a city, with its social connotations). The purity and devotedness of the bride are reflected in her attire" (Alan F. Johnson, *Revelation,* The Expositor's Bible Commentary [Grand Rapids, Mich.: Zondervan, 1981], p. 593).

Unbelievers, on the other hand, are compared to Babylon and to prostitutes (Rev. 17)—a sinful, fleeting relationship.

Question 7 "Alpha and Omega" are the first and last letters of the Greek alphabet. The words occur three times in the New Testament (Rev. 1:8; 21:6; 22:13). In 21:6, this phrase implies the eternal deity of Jesus Christ. He is the Alpha and the Omega—the Beginning and the End to everything. To better grasp the idea of completeness, compare "Alpha and Omega" to our "A–Z" concept.

Question 10 "Overcomes" is derived from a Greek word, *nikaō,* which also can be translated as "be victor," "prevail," "conquer." This same word is found in Revelation 2:11, 17, 26; 3:5, 12, 21; 21:7.

Question 12 Discuss how verse 8 could be explained to an unbeliever. What exactly is "eternal death"? Why do Christians need not fear it?

The core of the New Testament message is that Christ died for our sins, rose from the dead on the third day, and ascended to heaven. He literally overcame death for us.

STUDY 6
Everlasting Joy
ISAIAH 61:1–7

Purpose: To realize that true and lasting joy is not dependent on power, position, or possessions—it is a gift from God.

Question 2 "The setting continues to be the captivity, viewed in turn from Babylon (v. 1b) and the ruined Jerusalem (v. 3). To its first hearers the promise would be as literal as the earlier threat of exile (cf. 39:6); but as fulfilled by Jesus (cf. Lk. 4:21) it inaugurated the blessings proclaimed in the beatitudes and elsewhere to the downtrodden (*[brokenhearted]* is translated 'poor' in LXX, using the word found in Lk. 4:18; 6:20; 7:22), and particularly to those who mourn (cf. perhaps Am. 6:6). The *[release from darkness for the prisoners]* was to be spiritual, too, as John the Baptist had to learn" (*The New Bible Commentary: Revised* [Grand Rapids, Mich.: Eerdmans, 1970], p. 622).

Question 3 "Isaiah 61:1–2 alludes to the Year of Jubilee (Lev 25:8–55), when once every 50 years slaves were freed, debts were canceled and ancestral property was returned to the original family. Isaiah predicted primarily the liberation of Israel from the future Babylonian captivity, but Jesus proclaimed liberation from sin and all its consequences" (*NIV Study Bible,* p. 1545).

Question 5 The "crown" was a turban or ornamental headdress. "Oil of gladness" refers to the olive oil people used to anoint themselves on joyous occasions. A "garment of praise" was a beautiful robe that was worn on special days of thanksgiving. This phrase also refers to putting on a joyful attitude, as one would put on a piece of clothing. Such praise is "worn" so that everyone can see we have obtained victory in Christ, even over sorrowful circumstances.

The Lord comforts us through the indwelling Holy Spirit and through others who have received his comfort (see 2 Cor. 1:3–11). His comfort is not like the temporary hug of a friend, but serves two distinct purposes:

1. To support us in times of sorrow, regardless of its cause.

2. To turn our sorrow into joy and praise.

No heartache escapes God's notice (see Ps. 56:8 and Isa. 66:13). You may want to discuss how we can be instruments of God's comfort to one another.

Question 7 "Oaks of righteousness" represents each and every believer. We are planted by Christ himself and are to produce fruit for him. Why? To glorify God.

Question 11 In Revelation 1:6, John refers to the church as "a kingdom and priests." Commenting on that verse, Alan F. Johnson writes: "Of Israel it was said that they would be a 'kingdom of priests and a holy nation' (Exod 19:6; cf. Isa 61:6). . . . As Israel of old was redeemed through the Red Sea and was called to be a kingdom under God and a nation of priests to serve him, so John sees the Christian community as the continuation of the OT people of God, redeemed by Christ's blood and made heirs of his future kingly rule on the earth (5:10; 20;6). Furthermore, all believers are called to be priests in the sense of offering spiritual sacrifices and praise to God (Heb 13:15; 1 Peter 2:5)" (*Revelation,* p. 422).

Question 14 Close the study by reminding the group that this book's title—*Mourning: The Prelude to Laughter*—signifies the temporary nature of suffering, and the promise of a permanent state of joy when at last we meet our Savior.

Notes

Notes

Notes

Notes